Dear Parent:

Congratulations! Your child is taking the first steps on an exciting journey. The destination? Independent reading!

STEP INTO READING® will help your child get there. The program offers five steps to reading success. Each step includes fun stories and colorful art. There are also Step into Reading Sticker Books, Step into Reading Math Readers, Step into Reading Write-In Readers, Step into Reading Phonics Readers, and Step into Reading Phonics First Steps! Boxed Sets—a complete literacy program with something for every child.

Learning to Read, Step by Step!

Ready to Read   Preschool–Kindergarten
• big type and easy words • rhyme and rhythm • picture clues
For children who know the alphabet and are eager to begin reading.

Reading with Help   Preschool–Grade 1
• basic vocabulary • short sentences • simple stories
For children who recognize familiar words and sound out new words with help.

Reading on Your Own   Grades 1–3
• engaging characters • easy-to-follow plots • popular topics
For children who are ready to read on their own.

Reading Paragraphs   Grades 2–3
• challenging vocabulary • short paragraphs • exciting stories
For newly independent readers who read simple sentences with confidence.

Ready for Chapters   Grades 2–4
• chapters • longer paragraphs • full-color art
For children who want to take the plunge into chapter books but still like colorful pictures.

STEP INTO READING® is designed to give every child a successful reading experience. The grade levels are only guides. Children can progress through the steps at their own speed, developing confidence in their reading, no matter what their grade.

Remember, a lifetime love of reading starts with a single step!

*The editor would like to thank Craig Schermer
of the National First Ladies' Library for his
assistance in the preparation of this book.*

Text copyright © 2004, 2009 by Gibbs Davis
Illustrations copyright © 2004, 2009 by Sally Wern Comport

All rights reserved. Published in the United States by Random House Children's Books,
a division of Random House, Inc., New York. Originally published by Random House
Children's Books in 2004.

Cover photograph: AP Images/Alex Brandon.
Interior photographs: The White House, p. 5; Library of Congress, Prints and Photographs
Division: reproduction number LC-USZ62-960, p. 8; reproduction number LC-USZ62-7601, p. 14;
reproduction number LC-USZ62-113665, p. 20; and reproduction number LC-USZ62-111377, p. 26;
Cecil Stoughton, White House/John Fitzgerald Kennedy Library, Boston, p. 31; William J. Clinton
Presidential Library, p. 37; AP Images/Jae C. Hong, p. 43.

Visit us on the Web!
www.stepintoreading.com

Educators and librarians, for a variety of teaching tools, visit us at
www.randomhouse.com/teachers

Library of Congress Cataloging-in-Publication Data
Davis, Gibbs.
First kids / by Gibbs Davis ; illustrated by Sally Wern Comport.
   p. cm. — (Step into reading. A step 4 book)
Summary: Discusses what life is like in the White House and presents anecdotes about the children
of presidents Lincoln, Grant, Theodore Roosevelt, Coolidge, Kennedy, Clinton, and Obama.
ISBN 978-0-375-82218-6 (trade) — ISBN 978-0-375-92218-3 (lib. bdg.)
1. Children of presidents—United States—Biography—Juvenile literature. 2. Presidents—United
States—Family relationships—Juvenile literature. 3. White House (Washington, D.C.)—Juvenile
literature. [1. Children of presidents. 2. White House (Washington, D.C.).]
I. Comport, Sally Wern, ill. II. Title. III. Series: Step into reading. Step 4 book.
E176.45.D38 2004   973'.09'9—dc22   2003017476

Printed in the United States of America
11 10 9 8 7 6 5 4 3 2

STEP INTO READING®

STEP 4

FIRST KIDS

by Gibbs Davis
illustrated by Sally Wern Comport

Random House New York

Growing Up in the White House

Imagine your mom or dad is elected president of the United States. That makes you First Kid. Overnight, you're famous. And you're about to move into the White House!

The White House has 132 rooms (not counting secret passageways). The First Family lives in eight rooms on the second and third floors.

Lots of people visit the White House. Even famous people. First Kids get to meet their favorite sports and movie stars. At state dinners you might be able to say, "Please pass the salt, Your Highness."

Bored? The White House has a movie theater, swimming pool, and bowling alley.

Tired of waiting for the school bus? First Kids travel by limousine and private jet.

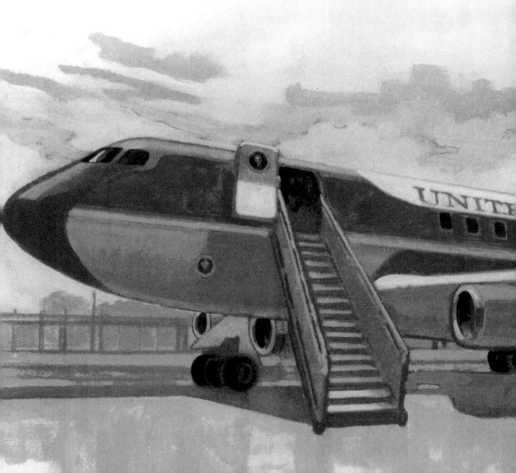

Can you guess the one thing First Kids *don't* have? Privacy. For safety, Secret Service agents follow them everywhere. They even have secret code names.

If you're shy, you might not like being First Kid. The whole world is watching you grow up. Your picture is in newspapers and on TV. Strangers know your shoe size!

Almost 200 children have lived in the White House. Some First Kids loved it. Others couldn't wait to leave. Would *you* like to live there? Read about some First Kids. Then decide for yourself.

1
Tad and Willie Lincoln
1861–1865

Abraham Lincoln and his wife had four sons—Robert, Edward, William, and Thomas. Mr. Lincoln said baby Thomas was as "wiggly as a tadpole." He called him "Tad." The nickname stuck.

When Mr. Lincoln became president, Robert was away at college. Eddie had died of diphtheria before Willie was born. So Willie and Tad had the White House all to themselves.

Willie and Tad were famous for their pranks. One time they rang for help in every room in the mansion. Servants ran in every direction trying to answer their call. Another time the boys drove their pet goats through one of Mrs. Lincoln's parties. The goats were pulling chairs with the boys on them!

No place in the White House was off-limits. Willie and Tad turned the mansion's roof into a battleship. They blasted the Cabinet Room door with a toy cannon. Tad set up a lemonade stand in the entrance hall and charged all the president's visitors for a drink.

Nothing could separate Willie and Tad. Except death. Willie came down with typhoid fever. At age eleven, he was the first child to die in the White House.

Nine-year-old Tad and his father became closer than ever. They even had their own secret code: three raps on the door, followed by two short bangs. No matter how busy, the president promised to always open the door when hearing the code.

One day Tad wanted to go for a drive. He knocked on the president's office door using the secret code. President Lincoln was in an important meeting. But he left it to join Tad and his pet goats for a carriage ride!

The secretary of war made Tad a lieutenant. He had his own Union Army uniform, which he called his "blues." Tad liked to march the servants up and down the lawn. They secretly called him the "tyrant of the White House."

2
Jesse Root Grant
1869–1877

Jesse Root Grant liked his father's new job.
The president of the United States got to
work at home. Before he was president,
Ulysses S. Grant had been a famous general.
He was away for years fighting in the Civil
War. Now father and son could spend more
time together.

Every clear night President Grant and
Jesse headed for the White House roof.
Jesse had a telescope. They stayed up late
studying the stars together.

Jesse's brothers were away at college. His older sister, Nellie, was busy with parties. Eleven-year-old Jesse could have been lonely. But he had lots of friends.

Jesse and his friends turned a White House toolshed into their secret clubhouse. They called themselves the K.F.R. Society. No one but them knew what the initials stood for. President Grant's guess? The Kick, Fight, and Run Society.

Jesse had bad luck with pet dogs. They
all died. Then someone sent him a huge
black Newfoundland named Old Faithful.
President Grant warned the servants, "If
this dog dies, you're all fired!" Luckily, Old
Faithful lived a long, long time.

Stamp collecting was Jesse's favorite hobby. Once Jesse and his cousin sent away five dollars for some foreign stamps. The stamps didn't come. President Grant asked a policeman to help his son.

The policeman wrote this letter:

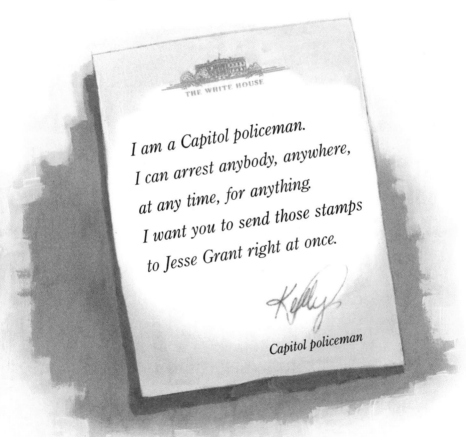

I am a Capitol policeman.
I can arrest anybody, anywhere, at any time, for anything.
I want you to send those stamps to Jesse Grant right at once.

Kelly

Capitol policeman

A few days later, the stamps arrived.

3
The Roosevelt Zoo
1901–1909

Theodore Roosevelt had six fun-loving children. They ranged in age from four to seventeen when he became president. The White House was one big playground to them.

The Roosevelts had more pets than any other First Family. The animals had free run of the White House. You might find a badger in the bathtub. Or a jumping kangaroo rat resting in someone's coat pocket!

One time Archie Roosevelt was sick
in bed with measles. He missed his pet
pony, Algonquin. His brothers and sisters
knew just how to cheer him up. They
snuck the pony into the elevator and up
to Archie's room!

Archie and Quentin Roosevelt formed the White House Gang. Six other boys joined them, including the vice president's son. Quentin was their leader. They had a clubhouse and a secret handshake.

The White House Gang was always getting in trouble. The boys skated down hallways and flicked spitballs at famous portraits. Archie liked sliding down the staircase on silver trays. Quentin was an expert stilt-walker.

Alice Roosevelt loved pranks as much as her brothers did. She had a pet snake named Emily Spinach. It was as skinny as her aunt Emily and as green as spinach. She hid her pet snake in her purse. At parties she let Emily slither out among the guests.

Alice became the most famous teenager in the country. Beautiful and playful, she was known as "Princess Alice." She even had a color named for her: Alice Blue.

4
The Coolidge Boys
1923–1929

Calvin Coolidge had two teenage sons, John and Calvin Jr. They went to school in Pennsylvania. The White House was their home only during summer and on holidays.

Nicknamed "Silent Cal," President Coolidge was a quiet man. His sons weren't so quiet. Calvin Jr. and John were typical teenage boys. Their nicknames were "Cal" and "Butch."

Life in the 1920s was wild and exciting.

But President Coolidge was a stern father. He wouldn't let his sons entertain friends or go to parties.

Mrs. Coolidge was more fun-loving. She wanted her sons to learn all the popular dances. A young dance-loving doorman named Johnson taught them to do the Charleston. The boys loved his stories about his "flapper" lady friends and the secret saloons called "speakeasies" in New York's Harlem.

Butch and Cal's first Christmas in the White House was filled with excitement. A giant spruce tree arrived by train. It came all the way from Vermont.

On Christmas Eve night a crowd gathered around the huge tree. Cal and Butch stood beside their father as he pushed a button. A thousand white lights lit up the tree. Everyone oohed and aahed at the dazzling sight. It was the First National Christmas Tree.

During summer vacation Cal and Butch liked to play tennis. One day Cal played barefoot and got a blister. It turned into an infection and he died. On the day of Cal's funeral all government departments closed down. Everyone mourned the president's son.

5
The Kennedy Kids
1961–1963

John Jr. was born right after the Kennedys moved into the White House. Everyone thought a new baby was good luck. The president nicknamed his son "John-John."

John-John had an older sister, three-year-old Caroline. She was nicknamed "Button-Nose." When Caroline arrived at the White House, it was winter. The chief gardener made a huge snowman to greet her.

Caroline and John Jr. didn't have to go far to get to school: just a short walk to the White House elevator and one flight up. Caroline joined eleven other first graders and John joined his nursery-school classmates at their own private school on the third floor.

The children's playground was near President Kennedy's office. Caroline's favorite game there was jumping on the trampoline. After recess their class liked to visit the president. His secretary always had candy for them on her desk.

President Kennedy traveled a lot. When Caroline's classmates heard his helicopter, everyone shouted, "Your daddy's home!" They raced to the window and watched him land on the White House lawn.

At story time Caroline always asked for horse stories. She had her own pet pony, named Macaroni. Her mother taught her to ride horseback.

Sometimes Caroline was allowed to go to White House parties. She helped her mother play hostess. Once the Marine Band played Caroline's favorite song, "Old MacDonald Had a Farm."

Caroline and John Jr. had thirteen cousins. During the summer they played together at their family home by the beach in Massachusetts.

In the winter, back at the White House, Caroline and John Jr. missed their fun-loving cousins. But Caroline and John Jr. had something even better. Their father was just down the hall for a bedtime story and a good-night hug.

6
Chelsea Clinton
1993–2001

Most First Kids have brothers or sisters to share the spotlight. But twelve-year-old Chelsea Clinton was an only child. (Unless you count Socks, her black-and-white cat.)

Chelsea's first few months in the White House were tough. It felt like living in a big museum. She missed her grandparents and friends back in Little Rock, Arkansas.

It was hard going to a new school. When Chelsea arrived, all the classroom doors had to be locked. Everyone had to knock and give their names before entering. Some of Chelsea's classmates were mad at her for all the new rules.

But after a while, everyone relaxed. There were no more locked doors. Everyone got to know the president's daughter. They found out she was a regular kid.

At school Chelsea played soccer and baseball. Math and science were her best subjects. One Christmas she danced in a ballet production of *The Nutcracker*. Her dream was to become an astronaut.

On Chelsea's thirteenth birthday she had a big slumber party. She invited old friends from Little Rock and new friends from Washington, D.C. The big mansion at 1600 Pennsylvania Avenue was beginning to feel like home.

The Clintons tried to protect Chelsea from the media. But they couldn't stop all the TV and newspaper reporters. Hurtful stories came out about her hair and braces. One time Chelsea fell asleep in church. A photographer took a picture of her snoring!

Chelsea got hundreds of fan letters. Kids from all over the United States tried to comfort her. They said they knew how she felt.

Sometimes Chelsea wasn't sure if people really liked her, or just liked being around the president's daughter. But she did know one thing for sure. She wouldn't give up being First Kid for anything!

7
The Obama Girls
2009–

When Barack Obama became president, ten-year-old Malia and seven-year-old Sasha were the youngest kids in the White House since the 1970s.

Like most sisters, they are different. Malia is levelheaded and calm. She enjoys soccer, ballet, and photography. Her father calls her Little Miss Articulate. Sasha is more easily excited and loves crowds. She likes singing and dancing.

Being First Kids has its perks. At the first-ever Kids' Inaugural concert, the star of Malia and Sasha's favorite TV show dedicated a song to them. When their favorite musical group—the Jonas Brothers—performed, the girls got up onstage to dance.

On their first night in the White House, the girls had a sleepover party with new classmates. They watched two movies in the White House theater. Then they went on a scavenger hunt. Hiding behind a door were the Jonas Brothers!

Malia got to redecorate her new bedroom. She called dibs on using Abraham Lincoln's desk for writing important history papers. "I'm going to sit at that desk because I'm thinking that will inspire big thoughts," she told her father.

Malia and Sasha have their own Secret Service code names. Malia is Radiance. Sasha is Rosebud. They call their Secret Service agents their "secret people."

When they moved into the White House, Malia and Sasha were the world's most famous tweens. But First Lady Michelle Obama made sure they stayed down-to-earth with her "Obama Rules":

★ *No whining, arguing, or annoying teasing.*
★ *Make the bed.*
★ *Get yourselves up and dressed on time.*
★ *Keep playroom toy closet neat.*
★ *Allowance for doing chores—one dollar per week.*
★ *No birthday or Christmas presents from Mom and Dad. [Santa gives Christmas presents, and the girls get birthday parties instead of gifts.]*
★ *Lights out at 8:30 (9:00 if reading).*

The Obamas are the first African
American First Family in the White House.
Children everywhere are watching Malia
and Sasha with pride and excitement as
they make history. Being a First Kid doesn't
get much cooler than that.